Original title:
Mars Bars and Lyrical Stars

Copyright © 2025 Creative Arts Management OÜ
All rights reserved.

Author: Wyatt Kensington
ISBN HARDBACK: 978-1-80567-835-9
ISBN PAPERBACK: 978-1-80567-956-1

Mellow Melodies and Chocolate Waters

In a land where laughter flows,
A river of cocoa gently glows.
With melodies that bounce and twine,
Chocolate whispers, all is fine.

The notes twirl like candy canes,
Tickling ears with joyful gains.
Bubbles of giggles pop in the air,
Sweetness dances everywhere.

Confectionery Constellations and Poetic Ripples

Underneath a sky so bright,
Candies twinkle, oh what a sight!
Each hue a wonder, a sugary song,
Guiding dreamers all night long.

Ripples of flavor spread like cheer,
Tickling taste buds, drawing near.
Every bite a galaxy here,
A chorus of treats, so sincere.

Rhyme Wrapped in Sweetness

Wrapped in laughter, rhymes take flight,
Chocolates melt in pure delight.
Jokes that stick like gum to tune,
Soaring high like a playful balloon.

Words of joy in every bite,
Crafted with care, so light and bright.
A sprinkle of fun on each page,
A confectionary dance on this stage.

The Starry Voyage of Sugary Thought

Set sail on a sea of whipped cream,
Chasing stars that giggle and gleam.
Every wave a sugar-filled jest,
Adventures await, just take a rest.

The captain's hat made of fondant dreams,
Navigating through whimsical streams.
A map written in marshmallow trails,
Where laughter echoes and humor prevails.

Candied Whispers and Celestial Dreams

In a galaxy full of treats,
Choco comets fly and greet.
Nibble on a starry bar,
As giggles drift near and far.

Sugar moons hover in cheer,
With candy clouds drawing near.
Laughter spills from every bite,
Galactic glee ignites the night.

Sweet Melody of the Infinite Sky

A symphony of flavors blend,
In outer space, where giggles send.
Sipping stardust, chuckling loud,
Floating free in a sugary cloud.

Chocolate rain and cookie streams,
Dance upon our wacky dreams.
Jokes and sweets, a cosmic mix,
Laughter spins in starry tricks.

Cosmic Bonds and Chocolaty Tales

A meteor made of fudge so sweet,
Whispers tales of spicy treats.
Riding beams of laughter's glow,
We taste the joy, feel the flow.

With every crunch, a silly laugh,
Galactic hugs in a chocolaty bath.
From the moon to Mars, we play,
In the candy cosmos, we frolic and sway.

Tastes of the Universe's Poetry

Stellar bites and giggly sips,
Words of joy roll off our lips.
Cosmic candy, a savory feast,
Creating smiles, to say the least.

With a sprinkle of humor, the stars align,
Nibbling notes that taste divine.
In this jest, we find our muse,
Galactic flavors we can't refuse.

Shimmering Cocoa and Starlit Melodies

In a cup of cocoa, swirls dance bright,
A galaxy of flavors, pure delight.
Sipping stars while moonlight hums,
Chocolate dreams, oh how it comes!

Frothy peaks like comet tails,
Sweet eruptions, no room for fails.
We laugh at cosmic candy trails,
With every sip, our joy prevails!

Cosmic Feasts and Poetic Treats

Gather round for a feast so grand,
A banquet where jibber-jabber's planned.
Twinkling cookies, candy galore,
With each bite, we crave for more!

The cakes leap high, they flirt and tease,
While jello wobbles like gentle seas.
A sprinkle here, a drizzle there,
Edible wonders beyond compare!

Sweets of the Universe's Storybook

Once upon a time in sugary lands,
Where gummy creatures danced hand in hands.
Chocolate boulders, frosting streams,
A fairy tale stitched with sweet dreams!

Lollipop mountains, licorice skies,
Where jellybeans twinkle, oh how they rise!
With each bite of wonder, stories unfold,
In the sweetest of tales, we're bold!

Star-Kissed Confections and Rhymes

Underneath the twinkling night,
Treats explode with pure delight.
Marshmallow moons and caramel comets,
Chewy spaceships, hop in the toilets!

Giggles echo in candy's embrace,
Sugar rush takes us to outer space.
With every nibble, laughter grows,
In a universe only sweetness knows!

Starry Night Confections

In a sky of sweets so bright,
Chocolate comets take flight.
With a sprinkle and a swirl,
Candy dreams begin to twirl.

Lollipop planets spin around,
In this sugary playground.
Giggles echo, laughter flies,
Joyful bites and tasty sighs.

Choco-Lyrical Odyssey

A journey through a candy land,
With each treat, a chewy strand.
Rhyme and chocolate blend just right,
In every munch, pure delight.

Marshmallow moons bounce and play,
While gumdrop sunbeams light the way.
Catchy tunes in every core,
With choco-verse, who could ask for more?

Interstellar Indulgence and Rhyme

Spaceships made of fudge and cream,
Glide through galaxies of dream.
Chocolate rivers, caramel tides,
In this sweet world, magic hides.

Witty whispers with every bite,
Punny stars shine through the night.
With laughter echoing near and far,
All aboard the sweet delight car!

Celestial Treats of the Poetic Kind

In a universe of crispy crunch,
A stellar feast for every munch.
Nibble rhymes, let laughter soar,
As candy comets crash and roar.

Jellybean wishes on candy skies,
Chocolate laughter, oh how it flies!
Every taste, a verse to share,
In this wonder, fun is everywhere.

Tasting the Night Sky

Under a blanket of sweet delight,
I reached for the heavens, with chocolate in sight.
Nibbling on dreams, I took a big bite,
The stars winked at me, oh what a night!

With every crunch, I soared up high,
As sprinkles rained down from the twinkling sky.
Floating on flavors, I began to fly,
Laughter erupted, oh my, oh my!

Galactic Rhymes and Chocolate Chimes

In the cosmos where flavors align,
The comets were dancing, how perfectly fine!
I juggled with moons, sweet berries enshrined,
And each rhyme was wrapped in a cocoa divine.

A symphony played, all the planets chimed,
With laughter and chocolate, the stars intertwined.
As the meteors fell, I knew it was time,
To savor the humor, the joy in the rhyme.

Chocolate Celestials

Celestial bodies made of fondant and cream,
Swirling around like a sugary dream.
With each bite I took, I heard a sweet scream,
As laughter exploded, oh how it did beam!

The milky way melted, a gooey delight,
Crispy surprises awaited me that night.
With every tickle of sweetness in flight,
The cosmos was giggling, full of pure light.

Whirling Confections in an Astral Dance

Stars twirled in wrappers, what a bizarre sight,
While cupcakes with frosting took off in their flight.
Each twirl brought a giggle, a sugary bite,
In a carousel of flavors, pure joy ignites.

The universe chuckled, as I danced with glee,
Candy canes swirled in sweet harmony.
With every spin, oh can you see?
A party of laughter, just you wait and see!

Whispers of Nougat and Stardust

In a galaxy sweet, where the flavors collide,
Choco rivers flow, on a nougat glide.
With each tasty bite, laughter takes flight,
Under twinkling skies, what a silly sight!

Aliens dance, with candy in hand,
Juggling caramels, oh, isn't it grand?
On cushions of fluff, as they giggle and cheer,
Sharing cosmic treats, spreading joy far and near.

Candied Comets and Serene Sonnets

Shooting stars sprinkle, a sugary dream,
With chocolate rivers, we float down the stream.
Each comet a bonbon, bright in the sky,
A serenade sweet, oh me, oh my!

Giggles erupt from the sugary gloom,
As flavors collide in a whirl of costume.
In this confectionery, laughter is gold,
With each silly tale, new adventures unfold.

Galactic Bites and Versified Delights

Nibbling on wonders from the cosmic tray,
Where bites burst with joy, in a whimsical way.
Rhymes dance in the air, from candy to star,
Each verse a treat, yes, we've come quite far!

Lollipop dreams and licorice skies,
With gumdrop wishes, oh how time flies!
In the swirling mess of sweet, sticky fun,
Each line a delight, till the day is done.

The Symphony of Cocoa and Cosmos

In the orchestra of sweets, the ciel conduct,
Cocoa beans play while the stars erupt.
Melodies twirl in a frosted embrace,
With every soft note, we all find our place.

The crunch of delight, a harmonic blend,
A whimsical rhythm that will never end.
All around, sugar floats in the breeze,
While laughter echoes, aiming to please.

Sweetness Amongst the Celestial Bodies

In a sky where snacks can fly,
A comet's got a candy stash.
Jupiter cracks jokes on the sly,
While Saturn makes confections crash.

Nebulae of nougat swirl,
As asteroids spin on a dime.
A Milky Way, with caramel,
Makes even black holes pause for rhyme.

Cosmic taffy stretches wide,
Eclipsing mates in sweet delight.
Planets bounce with every stride,
In this best sugar-coated light.

So here we laugh amidst the stars,
Sipping stardust, sharing cheer.
With every bite, we'll count the scars,
Of candy battles fought each year.

Rhymes of the Chocolate Cosmos

In the universe where cocoa flows,
Galaxies giggle, they cannot hide.
Chocolate craters, how the laughter grows,
As comets stick their candy-eyed.

The moons do dance, each bite's a tune,
On this cream-filled fun-filled ride.
Galactic glee beneath the moon,
With candy bars as our guide.

Shooting stars with wrappers bright,
Twinkling with a sweet allure.
In nebulae, what a sight,
Boosted by our sugar cure.

This cosmic circus, quite absurd,
Galaxy whirls with every cheer.
With parodies in every word,
Leave your worries, let them steer.

Galactic Sweets and Melodic Nights

Dancing comets, fizzing stars,
Strumming tunes of fudge and fun.
Galaxy piñatas full of jars,
Bursting laughter, never done.

A chocolate moon with sprinkles bright,
Invites a party in the dark.
While constellations sparkle light,
Sugar rush with every spark.

Crispy cosmos, munching bliss,
Notes will hum in every bite.
Every planet has a wish,
To join the laughter, what a sight!

So nibble stardust, play it sweet,
On this musical delight.
In this universe, we all meet,
With candy dreams our hearts ignite.

Decadent Verses in a Starry Sky

Up in the void where wishes linger,
A candy planet sings its song.
Wizards swirl with candy finger,
Whisper tales now buttered strong.

Fluffy clouds of sugary cream,
Twisting tales of cookie fights.
Each constellation's a sweet dream,
Crafted in these cosmic nights.

With a crunch and a fizz, we play,
Chocolate rivers take us high.
Floating through this soft ballet,
Our laughter echoes 'round the sky.

So take my hand, and let's explore,
This sugar-coated vast expanse.
In this universe, we'll implore,
To taste the joy in every chance.

Harmony in a Wrapper

In a universe of sweet delight,
Chocolate dances under pale moonlight.
Nutty whispers, caramel sighs,
Sugary dreams where laughter flies.

With each bite, the world aligns,
Twirling flavors, oh so fine!
Giggles echo in every chew,
Joyful hearts, and spirits too.

A crunch, a munch, the stars chime in,
Chasing worries, let fun begin.
In this galaxy made of treat,
Life's a party, oh so sweet!

Under the sky, where shadows prance,
Chocolate treats lead the dance.
Cosmic giggles, tasty affair,
In wrappers soft, our dreams lay bare.

Celestial Chocography

Stars melt down in pure delight,
Crafting tales in the cosmic night.
Cocoa comets blaze and tease,
Jokes and flavors float with ease.

A moonbeam smile, a nebula wink,
In the sweetness, we find our link.
Galaxies swirl, candy galore,
Each little morsel makes us roar.

Planets made of fudge and cream,
An interstellar sugared dream.
Beneath the laughing skies, we play,
Chocolate joy lights up the day.

With every bite, there's giggling glee,
Wrapped in dreams, just you and me.
In this cosmos, sweetly bright,
Humor flows like starlit light.

Chocolate Dreams Under Cosmic Flickers

Under starlit skies of dreams,
Chocolate dances, or so it seems.
Galactic giggles fill the air,
As cocoa clouds drift without care.

Nibbling on dreams, an astral delight,
Laughter twinkles, oh what a sight!
Wonders wrapped in soft embrace,
Joy spreads wide in this magical space.

Cosmo crunches, a sweet surprise,
Silly flavors, oh how they rise!
Taste the stars with every bite,
In a laugh-filled, scrumptious night.

Flickers of fun, in wrappers bright,
Joyful treats, a pure delight.
Moonlight melts in chocolate flows,
As happiness around us grows.

Celestial Confectionery Tales

In sweet tales spun from candy threads,
Laughter soars where joy is spread.
Stars of sugar, even bright,
Crafting fables beneath the light.

Chortles linger in creamy dreams,
As stars burst forth in cocoa beams.
Each tiny bite holds a mystery,
Wrapped in giggles and history.

Galactic flavors, a fine parade,
Chocolate treasures that never fade.
Heavenly mints, a whimsical race,
Tickling taste buds in this starry space.

From the cosmos comes the sweetest cheer,
A delightful burst year after year.
In confectionery bliss we bask,
As silly wonders joyfully ask.

Rhythm of Chocolate Under Cosmic Tides

In the night, candies gleam bright,
Jellybeans dance, what a sight!
Chocolate rivers flow with glee,
Under stars, so wild and free.

Pickles spin in sugary dreams,
Marshmallows float on moonlit beams.
With a laugh, we toss them high,
Confections burst, like laughter's pie.

Gummy bears in a comet's flight,
Cartwheeling past in pure delight.
Sprinkles rain down, like confetti wings,
Giggling under cosmic flings.

Choco waves surf through the air,
In this feast, we lose all care.
With every bite, joy ignites,
As we munch on starry bites.

Lyricism Lip-Synching to the Sweets of the Sky

Cotton candy whispers high,
Lyrical notes from clouds nearby.
Waffles sing in syrup's glow,
As gumdrops cheer, 'Come on, let's go!'

Cookies shout from chocolate hills,
With gummy worms that give us thrills.
Each verse is sweet, each rhyming bite,
In a sugary world, we dance all night.

Fig bars flip in a shiny twist,
Melodies swirl like a jelly mist.
Taffy stretching like silky dreams,
Life's full of fresh, playful schemes.

With whispers of fudge, we glide away,
In candy skies, we choose to stay.
Laughing through this candy chase,
In sweet harmony, we find our place.

Melodic Epidures of Confectionery Love

Chapters of nougat, love's sweet song,
Where caramel flows, nothing feels wrong.
Popcorn melodies burst like cheer,
In the land of desserts, there's no fear.

Lollipops share secrets anew,
With licorice twists bringing joy to view.
Pies that jiggle and dance with grace,
In this laughter-filled, sweet embrace.

Chocolate fondue fountains abound,
Each dip a giggle, a joy profound.
Honeycomb beats, so sticky and light,
Crispy crunches echo through the night.

Under candy canopies, we sway,
With sugar highs lighting our way.
In confectionery realms, we discover,
The fun in each sugary cover.

The Delicious Dance of Starlight

In a galaxy bright, candy takes flight,
A sweet little comet with chocolate delight.
Sprinkled with sprinkles, it twirls and it spins,
While giggling meteors join in all the wins.

Nibbling on nibs, the laughter ignites,
As moonbeams collide with sugary bites.
Wrapped in a foil that shines like the sun,
They join the parade, and it's all just for fun.

Bouncing around with a gift from the night,
The sugary stars dance with all of their might.
Galactic giggles echo back from afar,
Where laughter and chocolate are never bizarre.

So join in the joy of this sweet little show,
With every bright twinkle, oh watch how they glow!
For in this vast cosmos, it's perfectly clear,
A bite of pure bliss is what brings us all cheer.

Infinite Edibles and Lyrical Journeys

In a world made of fluff, where the chocolates all rhyme,
Lollipop verses spin tales in no time.
Nutty narwhals dive deep in caramel seas,
While candy cane quips ride the fizzy sweet breeze.

With pastries that echo like whispers of stars,
And cookies all dancing with luminous jars.
Bite-sized adventures in every big pack,
A giggly journey, there's no looking back!

Sprinkled with flavors that twist and delight,
The candy shop gleams like the stars of the night.
Swirling and twirling, oh what a grand sight,
With treats so enchanting, they ignite pure delight.

So grab your sweet snack and ride this fun wave,
With laughter and joy, let each moment save.
For in this universe of flavor and cheer,
Each bite's a new journey, let's hold it all dear.

Chocolaty Echoes Among the Stars

Under the blanket of the night sky above,
Chocolatey wonders are calling to love.
With nuts and caramel, they beckon us near,
Each bite a sweet echo, a sound we all cheer.

Fizzy little planets burst forth with delight,
As candy-coated dreams twinkle ever so bright.
The gummy bears giggle, the licorice sprawls,
While chocolatey blobs dance down candy cane halls.

In this sugar-filled space, every flavor can shine,
While laughter unravels like a tasty soft vine.
With each quirky morsel, the starlight unfolds,
A banquet of humor that never grows old.

So join the sweet chaos, take a bite and a chance,
In the universe's rhythm, let's all break and dance.
For life's like a treat, it's scrumptious and fun,
With every new nibble, our laughter's begun!

Galactic Delights and Dreamy Verses

In a universe swirling with colors so bright,
Galactic delights take us from day to night.
With fruity explosions and dips of sweet cream,
Every taste is a verse in our candy-filled dream.

Cotton candy clouds billow high through space,
While jellybean rainbows pop into place.
With every new nibble, a giggle takes flight,
As chocolate comets light up the night.

Sipping on starlight from cups made of fudge,
Our hearts become playful, there's no need to judge.
In the laughter of sweets, we find our true bliss,
A bite-sized adventure we simply can't miss.

So dance with the candies, let your spirits unwind,
For in this confectionery, pure joy you will find.
With each starry nibble and giggle so free,
We craft a sweet world, just you wait and see!

Heavenly Bars and Cosmic Rhythms

In candy realms up high, they float,
With wrappers bright, a tasty note.
Chocolate comets zooming past,
Nibbling stars in a cosmic blast.

Galactic giggles fill the air,
Sugar dreams without a care.
Twinkling treats, they dance and sway,
Laughter echoes night and day.

Floating sweets on stardust streams,
Nibbling joy, fulfilling dreams.
Each bite a spark, a laugh, a cheer,
In this universe, we draw near.

Crispy bites in a moonlit race,
Chocolate smiles on every face.
With cocoa clouds, we zoom above,
In this delight, we find our love.

The Sweet Lullaby of the Night Sky

Underneath the moonlit beam,
Chocolate rivers, candy dream.
Stars hum softly in the night,
Treats that bring us sheer delight.

Lumps of joy on every plate,
Sweetened giggles, childhood fate.
Crisp delights swirl all around,
With every bite, new laughs are found.

Fuzzy whispers of dreams on high,
Lullabies in the candy sky.
Fluffy clouds with a sugary twist,
Who knew sweets could be such bliss?

Cocoa kisses under starlight,
Delicious wishes take their flight.
In the night, we share our glee,
With every taste, we dance so free.

Edible Verses in Infinite Spaces

In a galaxy of sprinkled treats,
Verse and laughter mix like sweets.
Tasty tales in every bite,
Chocolate dreams that feel so right.

Light as air, with crispy bites,
Sugar highs on starry nights.
Stories spun with fudge and cream,
In every laugh, a tasty dream.

Nibbling words from cosmic pads,
Silly rhymes that make us glad.
In every corner of the sky,
Edible poems, oh my, oh my!

From Milky Way to candy lane,
Sweetened stories break the chain.
In this cosmos, joy arrives,
With each sweet verse, our spirit thrives.

Cosmic Currents and Sugary Whispers

Candy waves in the midnight glow,
Flowing gently, sweet and slow.
Starry whispers tickle ear,
As laughter sparkles all so clear.

Chocolate comets blushing red,
Cosmic giggles overhead.
Sweets that dance on lunar beams,
Ticklish joy in chocolate streams.

With every bite, a laugh we share,
Galactic treats beyond compare.
In this universe of sweet delight,
Our silly dreams take off in flight.

Sugar clouds in cosmic sway,
Whispers of fun, here we play.
Together under stars so bright,
In tasty worlds, we find our light.

Sounds of the Galaxy's Sweet Embrace

In the void, a crunch does sing,
Chasing comets, with funny bling,
A chocolate moon, so bright it glows,
Twirling aliens strike silly poses.

Floating treats in a cosmic dance,
Nibbled stars in a sugary trance,
Giggles echo from Jupiter's side,
Wobbling robots, joy they can't hide.

Asteroids with caramel cores,
Bouncing laughter, who could want more?
In this space, with candy delights,
Playful dreams launch to new heights.

Chewy Dreams adrift in Stardust

Sipping stardust through a straw,
Taste adventures that leave you in awe,
With frothy bursts of laughter galore,
Bouncing on bubbles, we twirl and soar.

Nebulae filled with marshmallow fluff,
Floating on giggles, ain't that enough?
Chewy comets fly, oh what a sight,
Dancing through cosmos, hearts filled with light.

Fizzy planets in a swirl of fun,
Every journey has just begun,
Waltzing with laughter among the stars,
Creating memories wherever we are.

Poetic Passions and Sugary Dreams

Ink flows like syrup, sticky and sweet,
Crafting verses, oh what a treat!
Words bounce like candy in a twist,
In this galactic, lyrical mist.

Witty rhymes in chocolate pools,
Where laughter's the answer, forget the rules,
Swirling ideas like caramel cheer,
Dancing with joy, we have nothing to fear.

Nonsense lines spin like a top,
On this journey, we'll never stop,
With sugary phrases that tickle the mind,
In a universe where fun is defined.

Starlit Choco-Scapes

Under stars, a chocolate sea,
Sailing sweet dreams, just you and me,
Crispy waves in a candy tide,
Finding joy in every glide.

Galactic giggles, a sugary song,
Joining together, we can't go wrong,
Nibbling clouds that fluffy and bright,
In this cosmic realm of delight.

Mixing flavors from every corner,
Becoming poets, world explorer,
Each sprinkle of laughter a galactic boon,
We soar among sweet treats, under the moon.

Verse Under the Velvet Sky

Beneath the twinkling night, they play,
With chocolate dreams that swirl away.
Jokes wrapped in wrappers, sweet delight,
Giggles bounce like comets, taking flight.

Silly wishes float on candy air,
As laughter dances without a care.
The stars wink back, in a friendly tease,
While the moon hums softly, aiming to please.

Bouncing like balls of fluffy fluff,
Each bite a giggle, never tough.
Shooting stars in their sugary dance,
Inviting all to join in this chance.

Under velvet curtains, laughter spills,
Sweets of joy, merely moonlit thrills.
With every crunch, the universe sings,
In the game of giggles, everyone brings.

Milky Way Melodies

Floating notes in the cosmic scene,
With every crunch, a melody keen.
Bubbles of laughter rise to the night,
  Mixing the cosmos in pure delight.

Strumming on stardust, a joyful tune,
As silly critters dance 'neath the moon.
Chocolate rivers flow with giggly glee,
A symphony sung by the buzzing bee.

Shiny wrappers crinkle in the breeze,
  Tickling fancy with playful tease.
Cosmic cupcakes, that twirl and spin,
Make wishes come true with a cheeky grin.

In a galaxy where laughter grows,
With every nibble, the fun just flows.
So take a taste of this bright delight,
And sing with the stars, oh, what a sight!

Caramel Cadence

Oh, the sweet tunes that caramel make,
Each lick and bite, a joyful quake.
Bouncing delight in every chew,
Creating a rhythm, that's funny and new.

Slipping and sliding on a gooey track,
Galloping giggles, there's no looking back.
Wobbling wonders beneath the sun,
A candy parade, oh what fun!

Syrupy laughter drips from the sky,
With each golden bite, spirits fly.
Nuts sprinkle joy in this silly song,
As we dance and munch, all night long.

With every bar, a story's spun,
Melodies of mirth, laughter begun.
In a candied world of pure delight,
Join the joyous rhythm, all through the night!

Sugar-coated Serenades

In a land where giggles tickle the stands,
Sweet serenades flow from tiny hands.
With each sugary note, come join the play,
As laughter pops like bubbles, hooray!

Coated in smiles, the fun never ends,
Twinkling like stars, our candy friends.
Chasing rainbows, we dance and spin,
Every sweet morsel beckons us in.

Here, the frolicsome melodies sound,
As we jump and jive, and spin around.
Rainbow sprinkles dance upon our feet,
In this confectionery land, oh so sweet.

So grab a treat as the night runs wild,
With each joyful bite, unleash your inner child.
In sugar-coated rhymes, we forever sway,
Sipping joy, night turns to day!

Chocolaty Echoes

In wrappers bright, they sing a tune,
Melting under the cartoon moon.
With every bite, a giggle flies,
Sweet surprises make us laugh and rise.

The crunch and munch, a tasty spree,
As flavors dance, we sway with glee.
Each nibble whispers silly dreams,
Chocolate rivers and marshmallow streams.

Cosmic Confections and Rhythmic Reflections

Galactic cravings with a twist,
Sugar comets, impossible to resist.
With a crispy snap and gooey core,
They bounce around, leaving us wanting more.

Stardust sprinkles, a sugary fight,
Candies shining, oh what a sight!
We laugh and munch, we giggle loud,
In this sweet universe, we're all so proud.

Celestial Sweetscape

Floating treats in the midnight sky,
Caramel clouds that make you sigh.
Popcorn planets and jellybean stars,
Unwrap the joy from afar.

Lollipop rockets zoom and glide,
Sugar-fueled laughter, oh what a ride!
The galaxies taste like a carnival fair,
In this sweet adventure, we all share.

Chocolate Lullabies

As chocolate whispers sweet, sweet dreams,
The world is wrapped in tasty schemes.
Cookies dance with a playful twirl,
In every bite, a choco swirl.

Giggles echo, laughter cascades,
In this dessert world, joy never fades.
Each nibble brings a charming cheer,
With chocolate lullabies drawing near.

Celestial Confections

In the galaxy, treats do shine,
Chocolate comets, oh so fine.
Sprinkled stardust on every bite,
Sugar-coated dreams take flight.

Milky Ways and fruity rings,
Whispering of cosmic flings.
Bite-sized planets in the sky,
Candy wrappers floating by.

Laughter echoes through the night,
Gumdrops twirl, a sugar flight.
Aliens munch with such delight,
Nibbling sweets, what a sight!

So grab a snack, let's dance and play,
In this world where candy sways.
Each bite's a cosmic joy to share,
With sugary smiles everywhere.

Starlit Sweetness

Twinkling lights and candy beams,
Under the moon, we chase our dreams.
Lollipop moons and starry pies,
Sugar sparkles fill the skies.

Choco meteors zooming fast,
A sugary trail, a sweetened blast.
Fizzy fizz drinks, bubbling cheer,
With every sip, there's fun so near.

Dance with glee, oh take a chance,
Choco bars begin to prance.
Wobbling stars in candy rains,
This laughter, joy, it gains and gains.

So let's indulge in every bite,
In this magical, tasty night.
With candy friends, let happiness flow,
In starlit sweetness, watch us glow!

Cosmic Crunch

Crunchy planets spin around,
Galactic snacks are to be found.
Puffed delights in chocolate moons,
Each one sings delicious tunes.

Asteroid bites, a crispy crunch,
Nibbling fast, we take the plunge.
Candy rockets shoot up high,
Zooming past, oh my, oh my!

Cosmic cereal in a bowl,
With milky rivers, what a goal!
Chocolate flares and nutty stars,
Fueling laughter from afar.

So gather round, let's munch away,
In this crunch-filled, playful sway.
A stellar feast for you and me,
In every bite, pure ecstasy!

Candy Dreams

Every night in candy land,
Sweet dreams drift like grains of sand.
Gummy bears on fluffy clouds,
Whispering tunes, oh how they crowd.

Chocolate rivers flow so free,
Where all your wishes come to be.
Jellybean fields stretch and sway,
In this land where joys hold sway.

Licorice lassos, pull us tight,
Swinging stars in joyful flight.
Marshmallow fluff, a soft embrace,
In candy dreams, we find our place.

So close your eyes and take a dive,
In a world where treats arrive.
Giggles echo; fun resumes,
In our sweet, sugary blooms.

Cosmic Gleams

Gleaming treats from far away,
Sugar sparkles come to play.
Twilight sweets that shine so bright,
Underneath the starry night.

Candy glows like nebulae,
Joining hands, we laugh and fly.
Fudge-filled stars in cheerful rows,
Celebrating as everyone knows.

Sippin' joy from cosmic cups,
Sugar rush, we can't give up!
Tickled by the taste of glee,
In this universe, we're truly free.

With every bite, delight's our theme,
In the starlight, we all beam.
So let's unite and share the fun,
In cosmic gleams, we're never done!

Chocolate Fantasies Beneath Astral Lights

In a galaxy of treats tonight,
I find a snack that feels just right.
Dancing comets, flavors collide,
With every nibble, joy can't hide.

Twinkling planets, my taste buds sing,
Like a meteoric chocolate fling.
A crunch, a melt, sweet dreams unfold,
Candy mysteries, daring and bold.

Asteroids filled with creamy delight,
Each bite transports me to new height.
Shooting stars of caramel cheer,
Indulging in joy, I shed a tear.

Galactic flavors swirl and twist,
Dessert adventures I can't resist.
Under celestial wraps of bliss,
Life's sweetest moments in each kiss.

Verse and Sweetness: A Cosmic Tale

Floating ship made of milk and zest,
Sailing through dreams, I feel so blessed.
With every rhyme, my heart takes flight,
Nibbling on wonders under the night.

Gravity's pull, but sugar stays light,
A caramel comet shines oh-so-bright.
Playful rhymes dance with fluffy cream,
In a candy cosmos, I chase the dream.

Words drip like chocolate, oozing with cheer,
A cosmic dance that draws me near.
I spin with laughter, skip to a beat,
In my sugar-laden, whimsical seat.

Celestial laughter fills the air,
Giggles of marshmallows everywhere.
Every line is a frosty treat,
In this universe, life's oh-so-sweet.

Recipes of Love Among the Stars

Baking magic on a cosmic rise,
Stardust whispers, love never lies.
A sprinkle of joy, a dash of flair,
In the milky way of sweet affair.

Mixing chocolate with a side of glee,
Galaxies swirl in a kitchen spree.
Kneading laughter, rolling smiles,
Crafting wonders across the miles.

Stars align as I taste the mix,
Crafting joy with a few sweet tricks.
Heart-shaped cookies from the dream machine,
In this recipe, love reigns supreme.

Sprinkling happiness, a twinkling sound,
Wonders of sugar, love unbound.
In every bite, a story waits,
Beneath the sky, my heart elates.

Gastronomic Echoes of the Universe

In kitchens blazing with a savory spark,
Sounds of sizzling sing in the dark.
Bubbles rise, flavors unite,
In this universe, we laugh with delight.

From onion moons to creamy sun,
Each dish tells tales of playful fun.
Echoing laughter with every taste,
In this cosmic dance, there's no waste.

Spices travel on a meteor trail,
Bringing laughter, never to fail.
With every whisper of culinary magic,
Life's simple pleasures feel so tragic!

So let's raise the spoons to joy's embrace,
Embarking on journeys through time and space.
In the cosmic kitchen, we're all a part,
Eating our way through the universe, heart to heart.

Lyrical Licorice and Stellar Serenades

On a night of candy dreams,
The far-off twinkle beams,
Chewy rhymes and giggly tunes,
Dance beneath the vibrant moons.

With a twist of playful flair,
Jokes are tossed into the air,
Licorice whispers, oh so sweet,
Underneath our happy feet.

Silly laughter fills the breeze,
Like licorice stuck in trees,
Stars sing out from skies so bright,
That bring us joy till morning light.

Starshine and Sweet Nothings

In a galaxy of treats,
Where cosmic laughter meets,
Sugar sprinkles fall like rain,
As we skip and shout again.

Chocolate comets fly on by,
Underneath the chuckling sky,
Jests wrapped snug in caramel,
Echo softly like a bell.

Gumdrops dance on candy clouds,
As we sing and laugh out loud,
Wishes twirl like taffy spun,
Bringing giggles, so much fun!

Sweets Beneath a Starry Canopy

Under the vast confection sky,
Witty chats and chocolate pie,
Gummy bears stacking high,
As fruity laughs go flying by.

Tootsie rolls in every shade,
To giggle and parade,
Lollipop wonders and silly pranks,
Floating high in joyful flanks.

Bright jellybeans ignite the night,
As we twirl with pure delight,
Sprinkled stardust on our nose,
With laughter through the cosmic prose.

The Cosmic Dance of Chocolate and Verse

In a universe made of cream,
Where giggles burst and gleam,
Chocolate rivers flow with fun,
As rhymes spun 'round the sun.

Bouncing off the milky way,
Jokes and pranks in grand ballet,
Sweets entwined with rhymes so bright,
Sparking joy with every bite.

Silly verses drift like dreams,
In a world that's full of schemes,
Cosmic dances, trails of cheer,
Wrapped in laughter, never fear.

Rhyme of the Chocolate Cosmos

In the sky made of nougat, sweets take flight,
Candy comets zoom past in the night.
A drizzle of caramel, a sprinkle of glee,
Bouncing between stars, oh what a sight!

Chocolate rockets launch high with a cheer,
Nutty misfits gather, bringing good cheer.
They giggle and wiggle on the cosmic stage,
As wrappers twirl in the galactic sphere.

Fudgy meteors crash, leaving a trail,
While licorice astronauts dance without fail.
The universe smiles with each tasty bite,
In this wacky world, we're destined to prevail!

So grab your sweet friends, and join in the fun,
With layers of laughter, we'll never outrun.
A carnival of flavors, laughter fills the air,
In this chocolatey realm, we're always young!

Galactic Treats and Rhythmic Beats

Under twinkling sprinkles, the fun begins,
With beats of the cosmos, the laughter spins.
Sugar's the language spoken all around,
Each rhythm a promise, together we win.

Jellybeans bounce like planets on a roll,
Fizzy drinks bubble, they ignite the soul.
Amongst the candy stars, we laugh and we sway,
In this delightful orbit, we reach our goal.

Pop rocks explode like fireworks bright,
Chocolate fountains flow, what a sublime sight!
Hop on the taste rocket, let's soar through the night,
With each burst of flavor, life feels just right!

So meet me in orbit, just take a sweet chance,
With gummy bears leading an intergalactic dance.
In this universe of flavor, we'll giggle and sing,
Wrapped in the sweetness, together we prance!

Stellar Sweets

A cosmic buffet of sugary delight,
Where marshmallow moons gleam through the night.
The chocolate rivers flow wild and free,
While lollipop trees bring smiles, oh so bright.

Frostings swirl, galaxies formed in a swirl,
Candy canes orbit, as the giggles unfurl.
A sprinkle of nonsense, a dash of pure thrill,
In the realm of sweet wonders, let laughter whurl.

Gummy aliens dance in a sparkling haze,
Their stretchy limbs prancing in sugary plays.
Beneath sugar stars, we twirl and we cheer,
For in this sweet haven, we banish dull days!

So take a big bite, let the flavors collide,
With friends by your side, let the joy be your guide.
In this world of sweet dreams, we'll feast without fear,
As the laughter surrounds us, we munch and abide!

Choco-visions in the Night

In the darkness of night, a vision appears,
A chocolate dreamscape that tickles your gears.
With each little munch, the stars start to dance,
In this wild wonderland, joy disrupts all fears.

A fountain of fudge, where wishes come true,
And candy-coated wishes dance under the dew.
Twilight treats twinkle, each bite brings delight,
With every sweet moment, the laughter renews.

Caramel rain showers, sticky and sweet,
Flavors collide in a whimsical feat.
Whipped cream clouds drift, sprinkle bliss from above,
As the night's soft embrace tugs us to the beat.

So take a step back, let the fun fill the air,
In this cherry-topped night, let go of all care.
We'll savor the moments, through laughter and games,
In this chocolatey cosmos, we happily share!

Constellation Confectionery

Under bright lights of the candy shop,
I pondered a world where sweet treats hop.
Chocolate comets, nougat beams,
Fizzing soda dreams burst at the seams.

Planets of peanut, constellations in cream,
Taste the cosmos, or so it would seem.
Sugar rush rockets, a delight to explore,
Asteroids made of jelly, who could ask for more?

Galactic goodies in a snack-filled race,
Orbiting flavors, a candy embrace.
Milky Way munches, oh what a sight,
With each bite I soar into the night.

Candy capers and chocolatey cheer,
Spacey delights, let's give a loud cheer!
Giggles and crunches as flavor takes flight,
Join in the fun, it's a sweet starry night.

Rhythms of the Red Planet

On a quest for snacks on a crimson globe,
Dancing with crunch bars, the taste buds probe.
Beats of sugar and swirls of delight,
Groovin' to flavors that take us to flight.

Fizzy meteors bounce, make the crowd cheer,
Sipping on stardust, nothing to fear.
Riding the wave of fruity delight,
A confectionery concert under the night.

Guided by giggles in a cosmic spree,
Seeking sweet treasures like candy debris.
Melodies bubble, cascading in fun,
Jiving with jellies until the day's done.

Cranking out laughter, our laughter's the bass,
Tasting the universe, it's a sweet embrace.
Riding the rhythms, we'll never be apart,
In this whimsical journey, it's all about heart.

Sweet Serenade in Starry Realms

Beneath the blanket where night meets delight,
Sweet harmonies shimmer, oh what a sight!
Chocolates are singing, nougats all sway,
A symphony of flavors that brighten the day.

Sassy little wrappers, they clap to the beat,
With a drum of the fudge that's oh-so-sweet.
Moonbeams are dancing on caramel flows,
Each note a treat, from my head to my toes.

Jazzy jellybeans in a festive parade,
Saxophones crunching in a grand escapade.
Melodies mingle with candies galore,
Twinkling like stars, who could ask for more?

Giddy and giggling, we sing out our song,
In this sparkling galaxy where we all belong.
The night is delicious, a taste we adore,
With laughter and sweetness, we happily soar.

Folk Songs of Flavor

Gather 'round friends, let's share a tale,
Of sweetened adventures that never go stale.
With caramel strumming and fudge on a fork,
We'll dance in a circle, our laughter the spark.

Bouncy toffees and fruity refrain,
Every note fills us with joy, never pain.
A harmony sweet with a sprinkle of zest,
On this candy-coated quest, we are blessed.

Flavors are echoes of stories untold,
Sung by the wrappers, both brave and bold.
Join in the chorus, let's savor the cheer,
In a world of delights, there's nothing to fear.

So raise your confections, let's toast to the night,
With giggles and sweetness, everything feels right.
In the land of the munchies, we all play a part,
With folk songs of flavor that sing from the heart.

Sugary Orbits and Harmonious Chimes

In a universe made of sweet delight,
Candy comets zoom in the night.
Chocolate moons glow with laughter bright,
Giggles echo in flights of kite.

Jellybeans dance on fluffy clouds,
Marshmallow dreams draw excited crowds.
Popcorn planets make the best of sounds,
As candy canes wrap around the shrouds.

Lollipop stars twirl in the breeze,
Sugar-coated wishes float with ease.
Sprinkle constellations that aim to please,
Candy cosmos, a sweet tease.

Dreams collide in sprightly runs,
Joyful hops and sugary puns.
In this realm, the laughter shuns,
Silly chums and candy buns.

Constellations Made of Chocolate Wishes

In the sky, where treats abound,
Choco-meteors begin to sound.
Gumdrops sprinkle love around,
A symphony of sweets is found.

Waffles shine like golden rays,
Fudge flows through the playful ways.
Stars dipped in syrupy glaze,
Create a joy that never frays.

Celestial sprinkles light the way,
To chocolate realms where children play.
With every bite, we delay the day,
As laughter fills the bright array.

Gummy bears with giggles are near,
In this world, we shed our fear.
Join the candy dance, my dear,
Under nights of joy and cheer.

Lyrical Delicacies in a Galaxy Far Away

In a distant place where laughter sings,
Cotton candy clouds embrace the flings.
Twirling with glee, imagination springs,
Sharing the joy that sweet freedom brings.

Banana-flavored stardust shines,
As melodies swirl in cocoa lines.
Guitar riffs dance with fruity vines,
Creating sweetness that aligns.

Each cupcake comet zips past me,
With icing trails of pure glee.
Cosmic cupcakes, come count with me,
Life's a treat, as it should be!

Bursting flavors in every beat,
With chocolate kisses, we are complete.
In this universe, we find our seat,
And laugh with friends, our very own fleet.

Flavorful Stars and Rhythmic Dreams

Up above, in a fizzy sky,
Flavorful stars twinkle and fly.
Cotton candy whims that make us sigh,
With laughter that beams and never dies.

Rhymes of caramel drip with style,
As joyous planets spin and smile.
Licorice ropes stretch across the mile,
With every hiccup, we go wild.

Tootsie rolls spark a playful cheer,
As we bounce along, staying near.
Witty wonders spark the frontier,
In a world where fun is always clear.

Luscious bites in a rhythmic dance,
With vibrant flavors, we take a chance.
Join the party, give sweets a glance,
In our hearts, they leave a prance.

Twilight Delights

In twilight's glow, sweet treats unfold,
A chocolate tale that's yet to be told.
With nougat dreams and caramel flows,
We laugh and munch as the evening glows.

Giggles erupt with each little bite,
Savoring joy in the soft moonlight.
Crunchy delights and bright-colored snacks,
Filling our hearts as we plot our tracks.

Crispy wrappers crinkle with cheer,
As friends gather round with no time for fear.
Beneath the stars, we share our delight,
In a world where laughter takes flight.

So let's dance with flavor, let worries depart,
In this late-night humor, we find our art.
With every chuckle and every shared grin,
Twilight's delights are a win-win again!

Orbiting Flavors in Sonic Harmony

Around the cosmos, flavors collide,
In spirals of fun, we take a wild ride.
Chocolate comets and bubbly delights,
We bounce through the stars with all our might.

Every bite sings a note, sweet symphony,
As we leap in joy, so carefree and free.
Nougat whispers twist in a giggling maze,
We burst into laughter, lost in a daze.

With each silly gesture, we dance in space,
Floating like candy, our happy place.
Sonic waves wrap us in tasty delight,
Orbiting flavors throughout the night.

So let's toast to joy with wrappers in hand,
Galactic humor, oh, isn't it grand?
In this cosmic playground, we love to explore,
Our laughter and sweets always ask for more!

Whispers of Flavor Under Nebulae

Underneath nebulae, flavors take flight,
With whispers of sweetness that dance through the night.
Chocolate rivers and caramel streams,
Fill our horizons with sugary dreams.

Beneath the starlight, we giggle and share,
Tasty concoctions that float through the air.
Nutty delights and sugary chips,
Each one a rocket, launching our laughs and quips.

In moonbeam reflections, we savor the fun,
With every sweet bite, our journey's begun.
Galaxies crumble with joy in our heart,
In whispers of flavor, we'll never part.

So let's twirl together, have candy-filled nights,
In misty embrace of galactic delights.
For in this vast sky, with laughter we soar,
Every sweet memory unlocks joy's door!

Symphony of Sugary Stars

In a concert of flavors, we sway and groove,
Each note of laughter makes our spirits move.
A symphony wrapped in a colorful blend,
With sugary twirls that never quite end.

Crinkle of wrappers, a rhythmic delight,
As we snack and joke under star-spangled light.
Toffee musicians join in the fun,
Creating a melody, we're never outdone.

The orchestra plays with a caramel kiss,
With every sweet sound, it's hard to miss.
Chocolate truffles dance as the trumpets play,
We clap our hands in a sugary sway.

So let's blend our laughter in this tasty score,
With flavors that echo forevermore.
In harmony's embrace, from dusk until dawn,
Our symphony of sweets will carry on!

Cosmic Melodies and Sugary Whimsy

In the sky where comets play,
Fudge and laughter lead the way.
Chocolate rivers, marshmallow trees,
Giggles dance upon the breeze.

Asteroids sprout gumdrop heads,
Whirling snacks, no life of dreads.
Sundaes spin with sprinkles bright,
In this world, all feels just right.

Shoot for joy, let worries fade,
In this galaxy, fun is made.
Candy stars shine through the night,
Every moment feels just right.

So grab a spoon, dip in the sky,
Taste the wonders, oh my, oh my!
With every bite and every tune,
Let's giggle to the candy moon.

The Sweet Side of Galactic Poetry

Floating in a sugary dream,
Chocolate fountains, a creamy stream.
Words like candy, bright and bold,
Stories sweet as tales of old.

Galaxies twinkling with candy bars,
Whispers of laughter from silly stars.
Sipping joy from a cosmic cup,
With every rhyme, we cheer and sup.

Floating treats in the starry night,
Nibbling dreams, all feels so right.
Each line written with a grin,
This universe coaxing us to spin.

So lift your voice to the twinkling skies,
Let giggles echo, let spirits rise.
In this sweet poetic dance,
We twirl in laughter, take a chance.

A Symphony of Stars and Cocoa

Under the blanket of the night,
Cocoa clouds drift, such a sight.
Each star twinkles like a treat,
Serenading with a rhythm sweet.

Comets zoom in a candy race,
Sipping laughter, a warm embrace.
Whipped cream frolics in the air,
While stardust sprinkles everywhere.

Guitar riffs played on peanut shells,
Echo through the sweetened swells.
Melodies burst like fizzy pops,
In this cosmos, joy never stops.

So come and join this galactic feast,
Where every lyric's a sugary beast.
Let's dance beneath the cherry trees,
In this sweet world, we're sure to please.

Dreams Wrapped in Toasty Apron of Night

In the oven of dreams, we bake,
Fluffy giggles, the joys we make.
The night wraps us in doughy cheer,
With every whisper, fun draws near.

Cookies dance on a milky way,
Pillowy puffs bring laughter's play.
Soft and warm, like a friend's embrace,
In this sweet world, we find our place.

Sprinkled wishes float through the skies,
Laughing echoes, the spirit flies.
With every bite, a memory blooms,
In this bright space, joy fills the rooms.

So feast on laughter, pure and sweet,
In the night's kitchen, we're well-complete.
With dreams all rising like bread in the sun,
Wrap your heart, the fun's just begun.

www.ingramcontent.com/pod-product-compliance
Lightning Source LLC
Chambersburg PA
CBHW071842160426
43209CB00003B/390